Matthew Legare

The management takes no responsibility for mental or emotional damage incurred by reading this book.
Thank you for your understanding.

copyright © 2018, 2021 by Matthew Legare

All rights reserved.

No part of this book may be reproduced or transmitted in any form or by any means, electronic or mechanical, except for the purpose of review and/or reference, without explicit permission in writing from the publisher. Brief passages may be excerpted for review and critical purposes.

Artisanal Gibberish logo design © 2021 by Matthew Legare

Cover design © 2021 by Niki Lenhart
nikilen-designs.com

Published by Unruly Voices
unrulyvoices.com

An imprint of Paper Angel Press
paperangelpress.com

ISBN 978-1-953469-53-3 (Trade Paperback)

10 9 8 7 6 5 4 3 2 1

*To Ami,
without whom I would be dead, in a ditch, on fire.*

BESTIARY BAFFLEMENTS

A Menagerie of Meaningless
Mammalian Malarkey

BEARS

Ursus means "bear" in Latin.
Arctos means "bear" in Greek.

The American Grizzly Bear's scientific name is *Ursus arctos horribilis*.
So a Grizzly's scientific name is "Horrible bear bear."

The Eurasian Brown Bear's scientific name is *Ursus arctos arctos*.
So a Brown Bear's name is "Bear bear bear."

So if you carried an Eurasian Brown Bear around, you would be bearing a *Ursus arctos arctos*.
You would be bearing a bear bear bear.

If the poor thing shed all its fur,
You would be bearing a bare bear bear bear.

This would make you a bare bear bear bear bearer.

If you were nude while engaging in this activity,
That would make you a bare bare bear bear bear bearer.

If you asked people to be patient with you while you were engaged in this activity,
They'd be bearing with a bare bare bear bear bear bearer.

CHOMSKY

You can buy a Noam Chomsky garden gnome.
It's a Noam gnome.

You can even buy one in Alaska.
That'd make it a Nome Noam gnome.

Plaster is pretty heavy, so they make it out of polystyrene now.
That's a foam Nome Noam gnome.

If you put it on a small flying device,
It'd be a foam Nome Noam gnome drone.

Much of this text has rhymed.
It's a foam Nome Noam gnome drone poem.

Otters

In the local zoo, there is an exhibit of otters.
These otters have a large, plexiglass tank to swim in.
This is known as the Otter Water.

Occasionally, samples of this tank's contents are sent to another zoo, contained in a ceramic vessel.
This vessel is made by the Otter Water Potter.

It's transported by the female offspring of the person who made the vessel, the Otter Water Potter Daughter.

Since these samples are rather important to research, the receiving zoo usually has someone keeping an eye out for the delivery, the Otter Water Potter Daughter Spotter.

If the receiving zoo has horses, sometimes the person keeping an eye out for the delivery does so on horseback, upon an Otter Water Potter Daughter Spotter Trotter.

Standing around in the sun waiting for this delivery will cause everyone involved to heat up, making the Otter Water Potter Daugher Spotter Trotter Hotter.

Because the pony gets overheated, it might be tempted to drink some of the sample from the other zoo, resulting in an Otter Water Slaughter, making the Otter Water Potter Daughter Spotter Trotter Hotter all for Naught...er.

CELTIC CONUNDRUMS

Scots and Irish Ideations
and
Silly Iterations

Celts

When Irish and Scots gather, it can be known as a Celt Fest.

If they get together to make cloth by matting fibers, that's a Celt Felt Fest.

If they take those fibers and make a sash, that's a Celt Belt Felt Fest.

And if that sash is decorated with contrasting fibers embedded in the mats, then it's a Celtic Felted Belted Felt Fest.

If detractors threw scraps at the participants during this, that would be a Celtic Pelted Felted Belted Felt Fest.

Probably enacted by a Celtic Pelted Felted Belted Felt Fest Pest.

But that's hot activity, which means the lout doing it would get overheated, resulting in a
Celtic Melted Pelted Felted Belted Felt Fest Pest, depending on how the Celtic Melted Pelted Felted Belted Felt Fest Pest Dressed.

Scotland and France

There is an arrangement between Scotland and France known as the Auld Alliance.

It has been going on for some time.
It is an Old Auld Alliance.

Scotland gets pretty chilly.
Making this a Cold Old Auld Alliance.

And the members of this alliance are considered to have great fortitude.
making this a Bold Cold Old Auld Alliance.

The members of this Alliance are given an emblem or insignia which indicates their participation in this arrangement. This emblem is known as the Bold Cold Old Auld Alliance Appliance.

The participants in this arrangement are asked to keep this emblem in view on their clothing at all times, in order to maintain the Bold Cold Old Auld Alliance Appliance Compliance.

Now while this is not a particularly expensive emblem, there are some who may aspire to rise in status, and will even go so far as to purchase a shinier emblem, getting a Gold Bold Cold Old Auld Alliance Appliance, which in some case could be seen as Gold Bold Cold Old Auld Alliance Appliance Compliance Defiance!

But that kind of leaping above your status could put one in debt, resulting in some poor sod engaging in Gold Bold Cold Old Auld Alliance Appliance Compliance Defiance Refinance.

It's a deep shame to have to pawn this emblem, because no one wants to see someone wandering about with a Sold Gold Bold Cold Old Auld Alliance Appliance, in Defiance of the Refinance, making the previous owner of the Sold Gold Bold Cold Old Auld Alliance Appliance Compliance Defiance Refinance have to quit the clan and try pants.

Lakes

There are no lakes in Scotland,
This is because in Scotland, a lake is called a loch.
The Scottish are a robust, hearty people; they love no better exercise than to walk a loch.
However, Scots are also very territorial.
And they, if provoked, will take effort to block a loch walk.
Which will doubtless provoke their neighbors.
Who would then take great glee to mock the blocked loch walk.
This happens rather a lot, as Highlanders are a risible bunch.
So much so that they will often don special clothing to harass their neighbors.
So you might see one in a blocked loch walk mocking frock.
This is actually rather popular in the area,
and you're likely to find Scotland chock-a-block in Scots in blocked loch walk mocking frocks.

… from which we get the phrase, "Get the frock out of here!"

Sporrans

If you've been in Scotland for any amount of time, you'll note that Scotsmen tend to have a sort of pouch positioned rather strategically on the front of their kilts.

This pouch is known as a sporran.

Now, most Scotsmen like to make 'em ornate, to prevent themselves from having a borin' sporran.

That being said, on more than one occasion I've heard Scotswomen profess their appreciation of a more spartan pouch, which tells me that there's some out there who are adorin' a borin' sporran, and that they'd be quite forlorn if someone were deplorin' the borin' sporran they be adorin'.

In fact, being the strong-willed lot they are, I think that if they found out that someone were deplorin' the borin sporran they be adorin, they'd be adorin that forlorn borin' sporran more an' more'n.

ENGLISH EXCESSES

Bombastic British-Based Babblings

Saint George

Legend has it that Saint George killed a dragon with his sword.

And the place where the sword was made ... is now known as the Saint George Forge.

This blacksmithy is located in a deep valley.

This is the Saint George Forge Gorge.

Next to it is a shed, which is of course the Saint George Forge Gorge storage.

Now, many pilgrims would come to this place, thinking it holy, and they'd be rather strapped to find something to eat ... resulting in Saint George Forge Gorge storage forage.

Eventually some enterprising landlord set up a small kitchen and started serving oatmeal to the pilgrims.

This is now known as Saint George Forge Gorge storage forage porridge.

Garter

April 23rd is Saint George's Day. This is the day when new appointments to the Order of the Garter (one of the highest orders of chivalry in England, founded by King Edward III in 1348) are announced.

These initiates into the Order might be known as Garter starters.

Both chivalry and wit are valued as criteria for membership into the Order.

These are the smarter Garter starters.

… as is creativity, so these individuals are, in fact, the artier smarter Garter starters.

As I said, this is the highest order of chivalry in King Henry's England … so these appointees must be very, very brave.

They are the heartier artier smarter Garter starters.

And while it is a solemn order, there is a great deal of celebration after the ceremony.

Making these the "party-hearty" heartier artier smarter Garter starters.

So much so that, sadly, sometimes these men revel a bit too much and must be hauled back to the castle… in a "party-hearty" heartier artier smarter Garter starter cart by a "party-hearty" heartier artier smarter Garter starter carter.

Occasionally, such as after a good hard war, there are a number of new appointees, which means we need more than one "party-hearty" heartier artier smarter Garter starter cart, and traffic gets a bit confused in the return to court, so that we have a "party-hearty" heartier artier smarter Garter starter cart athwart another "party-hearty" heartier artier smarter Garter starter cart resulting in the loss of one of these vehicles, making for a "party-hearty" heartier artier smarter Garter starter carter martyr.

The poor pilot of the lost cart must try and trade the wreckage of his vehicle for something of more value which may be obtained through "party-hearty" heartier artier smarter Garter starter carter martyr barter, which he could use to get another vehicle at the "party-hearty" heartier artier smarter Garter starter carter martyr barter cart mart.

Henry VIII

Our King Henry VIII is currently between wives. He's actively hunting for a new bride.

He is a Tudor suitor.

He's been without something to, um, frolic with for a while ... and that can make a man rather randy.

That makes him a lewder Tudor suitor.

And of course, he's also a little depressed about the whole thing.

Which makes him a broodier lewder Tudor suitor.
All of this gets his sister (HRH Margaret, Queen of Scotland etc.) rather annoyed. They argue sometimes.

So she's feudin' with a broodin' lewdin' Tudor suitor.

So much so that she asked some artisans to carve a bust of her brother out of walnut so she can yell at THAT in the privacy of her own chambers.

She's feudin' with a wooden broodin' lewdin' Tudor suitor.

Now we all know that King Henry VIII was fond of the hunt ... for just about anything. So he might ride off and fire arrows at stuff. He might even use a cannon for hunting!

Then Queen Margaret would be feudin' with a wooden shootin' broodin' lewdin' Tudor suitor.

Unfortunately, wood has a tendency to rot, given time. So you have to protect it, through a process known as "pickling" or even coating it with a thin layer of varnish. Sometimes that varnish takes an azure hue.

So Her Majesty would be feudin' with a stewed 'n' blued wooden shootin' broodin' lewdin' Tudor suitor.

Now if someone went and painted graffiti on it …

She'd be feudin' with a stewed, blued, and tattooed wooden shootin' broodin' lewdin' Tudor suitor.

Now, let's be honest here, metal is more durable than wood, and Queen Margaret did have a metal bust of her brother once … which looked even more lecherous than the walnut one …

But someone looted the pewter shootin' broodin' lewdin' Tudor suitor, which is why she's now feudin' with the stewed, blued, and tattooed wooden shootin' broodin' lewdin' Tudor suitor.

Now that could have been avoided if she had eschewed the pewter shootin' broodin' lewdin' Tudor suitor, but the brutal lootin' mooted the forsootin' truth of the prudish eschewin' which led to the feudin' with the stewed, blued, and tattooed wooden shootin' broodin' lewdin' Tudor suitor.

HOLIDAY HOGWASH

Festive Far-Fetched Fiddle-Faddle

Ghosts

In the middle of autumn, a time comes for the consideration of ghosts and spectres.
If such a supernatural creature visits your residence, it might be considered a 'haunt'.

Now not everyone might want a haunt, but some folks might well want to flaunt their haunt.

Particularly if it's a relative. Like your mother's sister.
You might well want to flaunt your aunt's haunt.

it might be even more desirable should your mother's sister have died early.
Then, you might well want to flaunt your enfant aunt's haunt.

Not everyone understands this sort of desire, which could lead to teasing.
You'd find someone might taunt you if you want to flaunt your enfant aunt's haunt.

This might put you off your feed … causing you go gaunt from the taunt for the want of your enfant aunt's haunt.

Corn

In the Taino language, corn is called *maize*.

In the autumn months, some farmers let their maize grow tall and then carve pathways in amongst the stalks.

This would be a maize maze.

They can get pretty intricate, resulting in an amazing maize maze.

You can find a great many of these things in autumn, as it is a bit of an amazing maize maze craze.

So many, in fact, that you might become rather sick of the whole thing, and may just want to burn all of the darn things down.

Yes, you might just want to set ablaze the amazing maize maze craze.

But, as it is seasonal, you just have to remember that this too shall pass, and we will all get through this ablaze amazing maize maze craze phase.

Yule

At Christmas time, people often burn what's known as a yule log.

The device used to adjust this log in the fireplace is known as the yule tool.

Since there's not a lot of use for this device over the rest of the year, these devices are often stored in a common location, known as the yule tool pool.

These devices must be carefully maintained and stored to ensure their usefulness over several years, and that's known as the yule tool pool rule.

Every so often, one such device is particularly well-maintained and as such, stands out as the jewel of the yule tool pool rule.

NAUTICAL NONSENSE

Seafaring Senseless Slobber

SHIPS

A ship is a water-going vessel.

When such a vessel is used to deliver trade goods, it is called "shipping".

Therefore, a water-going vessel which delivers trade goods is a shipping ship.

These vessels come from a facility which manufactures water-going vessels involved in trade.
This is a shipping ship shipyard.

Delivering the vessel from the facility requires another vessel …
Or, a shipping ship shipyard ship shipping ships from the shipping ship shipyard.

Seagoing vessels are often thought to have human emotions, like love.

And if two of these vessels involved in transporting vessels involved in delivering trade goods were thought to be romantically involved, then you'd be shipping shipping ship shipyard ships shipping ships.

Kraken

If you're a pirate, you know that at some point, you're likely going to have to
RELEASE THE KRAKEN.

The problem is, once you've released the dang thing, sooner or later you're going to have to go after it so you can put it away.

You're going to have to do some kraken trackin'.

When you do so, you're going to get hungry. You're going to want to eat.
You're going to do some kraken trackin' snackin'.

Of course, since you're on the move, you'll have to take your provisions with you,
so you're going to be kraken trackin' snackin' packin'.

And you want to make sure you have enough provisions. Maybe a bit more than you think you need,
because you don't want to be lackin' in your kraken trackin' snackin' packin'.

Because if you were, you'd likely be derided. People might mock you.
Some wag would be giving you flack for your lackin' in kracken trackin' snackin' packin' .

And, if you hadn't eaten enough, you'd be a bit slow on the uptake.
So you'd be taken aback by the flack for your lackin' in kracken trackin' snackin' packin'.

And being peckish, you'd also be a bit cranky. You'd probably pretty salty.

So you'd be wanting to give someone a smackin' and maybe a shellackin' after being taken aback by the flack for your lackin' in kraken trackin' snackin' packin'.

Now that sort of beating takes some skill. You might get good at it.

So people would say you had a knack in smackin' and shellackin' the hack who took you aback for the flack for your lackin' in kracken trackin' snackin' packin'

Cleats

A cleat is a device on a ship to secure a rope.

A high-quality device to secure a rope would be an elite cleat.

If you had many of these devices on your ship,
your ship would be replete with elite cleats.

This level of quality might attract other ships to sail in your company.
so that you'd have a fleet replete with elite cleats

And if you were very successful, and attracted a bunch of boats with a bunch of these devices,
You would be able to accrete a suite of fleets replete with elite cleats.

With all that expensive equipment on those boats, you'd have to keep them tidy.
So you'd have a very neat accreted suite of fleets replete with elite cleats.

Now, to pay for all of this, you'll need to have good contacts in the business.
You'll need to do some networking.

You might arrange for a meet-and-greet for the neat accreted suite of fleets replete with elite cleats.

Because many would consider it a treat to have a meet-and-greet for the neat accreted suite of fleets replete with elite cleats.

It would certainly beat some off-the-street effete cheat's backstreet not-so-neat fleet that could not compete, causing him to beat a deceitful retreat.

MISCELLANY

Which is Hard
to Properly Rhyme

Holy Water Cannon

The Pope has a water cannon in the Vatican, for the blessing of large crowds.
It is a holy water cannon.
He has blessed this device.
It is a holy holy water cannon.
He blessed this device very thoroughly.
It is a wholly holy holy water cannon.
This blessed device has been well-documented.
So we have a wholly holy holy water cannon canon.
Sadly, the blessed device has sprung a few leaks.
So we have a holey wholly holy holy water cannon canon.
Due to the leaks, the Pope has had an additional reservoir installed on it.
Which makes it a holey wholly holy holy water can-on cannon canon.

Hurdy Gurdy

I bought a hurdy-gurdy.
I just want that to sink in.
I BOUGHT A HURDY-GURDY.
It is an aesthetically pleasing instrument.

It's a purdy hurdy-gurdy.
It is chased with elaborate calligraphy along the casing.
It's a wordy purdy hurdy-gurdy.

Some of the calligraphy is in fact quotations from love poetry.
It's a flirty wordy purdy hurdy-gurdy.
Now, when I take this out to perform -- as no doubt I will do -- I will have to be careful with how I treat it.
I do not want it to become mussed.
No one wants a dirty flirty wordy purdy hurdy-gurdy.

My biggest concern is that as the instrument becomes popular, the festivals I perform at will become oversaturated with these instruments.
Perhaps up to thirty dirty flirty wordy purdy hurdy-gurdys.

And if they're all performing in the same place at the same time, they're all bound to get a bit rude.
Then we'd be stuck with thirty shirty dirty flirty wordy purdy hurdy-gurdys.

And I feel it would fall unto me to try and wrangle all these instruments together. Possibly playing a common piece in which all these instruments played in accompaniment to something else entirely.

I'd probably have to do a bunch of them.

Those would comprise the thirty shirty dirty flirty wordy purdy hurdy-gurdy concerti.

Outhouses

Another word for an outhouse is a crapper.
If it's a particularly well-kept outhouse, then it is a dapper crapper.
If this well-kept outhouse has a lid on the hole, that'd be a dapper crapper flapper.
And if that lid had a paper band on it indicating that it had been sterilized for your convenience, that would be a dapper crapper flapper wrapper.
Now, if someone kept sneaking in to remove that band, he'd be a dapper crapper flapper wrapper scrapper.
And would be pursued by a dapper crapper flapper wrapper scrapper trapper.
Said trapper would have to keep close surveillance on the paper band, by using a camera, or a dapper crapper flapper wrapper scrapper trapper snapper.

Purse

My friend has a purse.

Inside this purse is a smaller purse for coins and such
...
It is a recursive purse.

When she makes a payment using coins from the smaller container ...
It is a recursive purse disbursement.
This makes her a recursive purse disbursement bursar.

Some people don't like to be paid in change, and thus, they would be averse to a recursive purse disbursement by my friend the recursive purse disbursement bursar.

So she has taken pains to be as genteel about it as possible and even made it rhyme
so as not to rile the adverse during a recursive purse disbursement, she has rehearsed a recursive purse disbursement bursar verse.

Vacuum

A device which uses suction to clean things is a vacuum cleaner.

When you clean a vacuum cleaner, you become a vacuum cleaner cleaner.

If you then take a shower to clean all the dust off yourself, the shower becomes a vacuum cleaner cleaner cleaner.

Then you have to scrub the shower, which makes you a vacuum cleaner cleaner cleaner cleaner.

And if you use a vacuum cleaner to clean the shower, it becomes a vacuum cleaner cleaner cleaner cleaner vacuum.

About the Author

Matthew Legare (aka "Tobias the Adequate") is what happens when you tell someone they can be anything they want to be — but provide no further guidance. A performer and creator of "stuff" since he was able to stand upright, he can check off the boxes for "actor", "writer", "director", "renter of fishing boats", "painter of bathrooms", "wrangler of technology", and a number of other jobs which look good in an author's biography.

Unable to stop making stuff up (he's tried; we checked), Matthew is credited (or blamed) with a number of radio plays and spoken-word performances at fairs, festivals, and themed gatherings. Since so many people responded to "I'm a magician." with "Oh? What instrument do you play?", Mr. Legare has branched into geeky, nerdy, goofy music with his "Troubadork" show, streaming regularly and coming to the aforementioned gatherings.

Matthew lives in an undisclosed location in San Antonio, Texas, with his extremely patient and supportive partner, Ami, and somewhere between zero and too many cats.

www.ingramcontent.com/pod-product-compliance
Lightning Source LLC
Chambersburg PA
CBHW021452070526
44577CB00002B/373